Make Your Own Art

Paper Folding

Sally Henry

PowerKiDS press™

New York

Published in 2009 by The Rosen Publishing Group, Inc.
29 East 21st Street, New York, NY 10010

Editor: Alex Woolf
Designers: Sally Henry and Trevor Cook
Consultant: Daisy Fearns
U.S. Editor: Kara Murray

Picture credits: Sally Henry and Trevor Cook

Every attempt has been made to clear copyright.
Should there be any inadvertent omission,
please apply to the publisher for rectification.

Library of Congress Cataloging-in-Publication Data

Henry, Sally.
  Paper folding / Sally Henry.
      p. cm. — (Make your own art)
  Includes index.
  ISBN 978-1-4358-2507-9 (library binding)
  ISBN 978-1-4358-2640-3 (pbk)
  ISBN 978-1-4358-2652-6 (6-pack)
  1. Paper work—Juvenile literature. I. Title.
TT870.H427 2009
736'.98—dc22
                                        2008004524

Manufactured in China

Contents

BANG

Introduction

The art of folding paper is almost as old as paper itself. Paper was invented in the East, and there are many ancient paper-folding designs. Old and new designs all share the same basic requirements for success.

Paper

Use ordinary, colored letter-size office copier paper, unless the directions say otherwise. It's fun to use all kinds of paper, though. Try patterned paper, such as wrapping paper. It's usually printed on one side and plain white on the other. Colored art paper comes in sizes much bigger than office paper, so it's good for a special activity.

To make the flowers on page 16, you can use tissue paper or crepe paper.

Tissue paper comes in bright colors. It is thin enough to let light shine through it, making the colours bright but natural looking.

Crepe paper is thicker than tissue paper and is made with lots of tiny creases. This means that by gently pulling at it, you can make the paper no longer flat but curved.

Paper often folds best in one direction. If you find it hard to make a clean fold, this may be the reason. Experiment with some scrap.

Always ask an adult to help you when you are using sharp objects, such as scissors.

Fold

The dotted line shows where the fold should be made. The arrow shows which direction to make the fold. There is usually an edge or a point that the folded part has to meet.

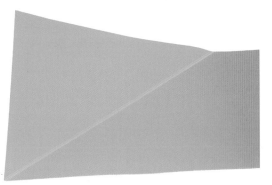

Crease

Make a fold in a sheet of paper and open it up again. The mark left is a crease. Depending on the design, you can use this as a fold later in the construction, or you might just use it as a guide to get other folds in the right place.

Burnished fold

When you want a fold to be really crisp and lay flat, or a crease to be very clear, use a tool to burnish the fold. Make the fold very carefully, and check that it is in the right place. Then gently rub down the fold using a tool such as a ruler or the back of a spoon.

Tricky folds

Be careful when one end of
the fold meets another
fold. Try to make this
a crisp angle.

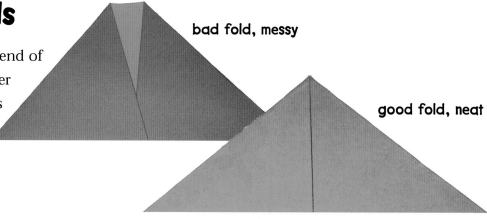

bad fold, messy

good fold, neat

Curling paper

Sometimes you may want to make your paper
bend or curl. You can make paper gently curl by
wrapping it around a pencil.

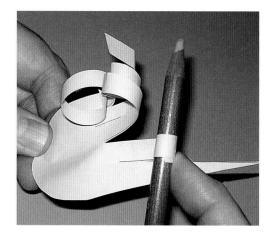

Steadily pulling it
under the edge of a
ruler will make a
tighter curl, depending
on how hard you
pull it.

Lining paper

For really large folding projects,
and for making hats, lining paper
is ideal. It comes on rolls and you can
buy it quite cheaply at DIY stores.

Glue

You may need one of two sorts of glue. The sort that comes as a **glue stick** is ideal for sticking flat pieces of paper to paper. Place the piece to be glued facedown on a clean piece of scrap paper and apply the glue evenly, working towards the edge. You can use it for putting the bits of decoration on the snappers (see page 22).

Rubber cement that comes in a tube is best for sticking odd-shaped bits together and for sticking paper to other materials. Use it for sticking the leaves to the stems of the flowers (see page 16). This glue dries clear but try to avoid getting it on the front of your work. Use a matchstick to spread this glue on small things.

Decorating paper

If you want to paint patterns or designs on your paper folding, do it before you start, not on the finished work. This is much neater and will make the result much better!

Windmills

The paper windmill is an old favorite. It's so simple to make. Enjoy creating our model with your friends.

10 MINUTES

1 MINUTE

You will need:

- *Thin card stock or colored paper, pins, sticks*
- *Scissors, ruler or triangle, pencil*

What to do...

Find a table to work on. Measure a square
8 x 8 inches (20 x 20 cm) on your card stock.

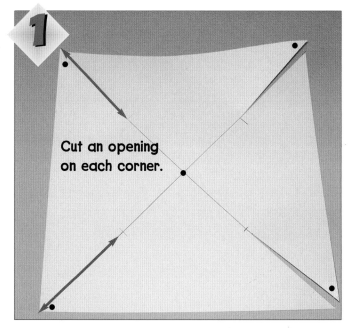

Draw diagonal lines from corner to corner. Use scissors to cut 4 inches (10 cm) along the lines. Make a small hole in the center and to the side of each triangle.

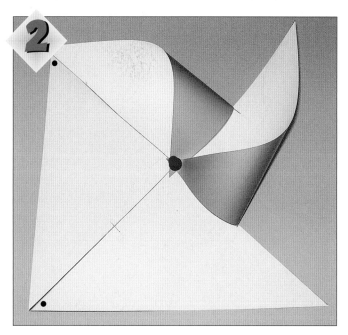

Put a pin through one corner hole and bend the paper over to the middle.

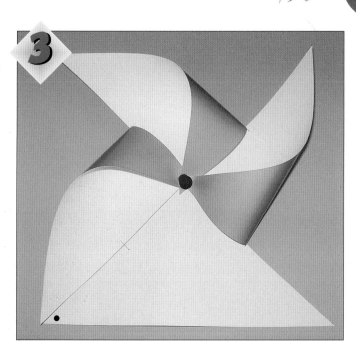

When you have gathered all four corners together, push the pin through the center hole and press it into the top of a stick. Fix the pin so the windmill turns freely.

It's best to decorate your windmill before you put it together.

Gift Boxes

A folded box that you've made yourself is a great way to present gifts of candies or small toys. Make this design without using glue. You'll be surprised how useful it can be.

You will need:

- *Thin card stock or thick paper*
- *Scissors, ruler*
- *Wrapped candies (optional)*

5 MINUTES

What to do...

Start with a piece of paper 6 x 6 inches (15 x 15 cm). Fold the short sides together and make a light crease.

0 MINUTES

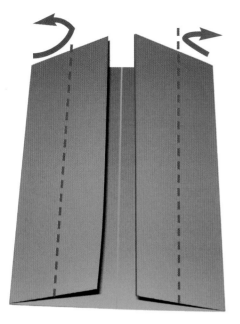

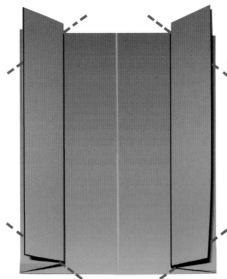

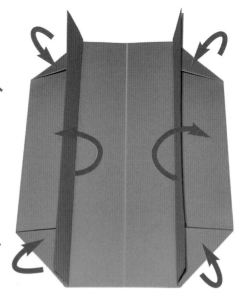

1   Open the paper out and fold the short sides in to meet the center crease.

2   Fold back the pieces to the edges. Fold the four corners into the creases.

3   Fold the top pieces back and burnish them down firmly. Turn the paper over.

6   Add wrapped candies.

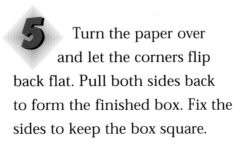

4   We have bent the bottom part up. Now bend the top part down at the crease so that you see squares at the corners.

5   Turn the paper over and let the corners flip back flat. Pull both sides back to form the finished box. Fix the sides to keep the box square.

Use patterned paper too!

High Fliers

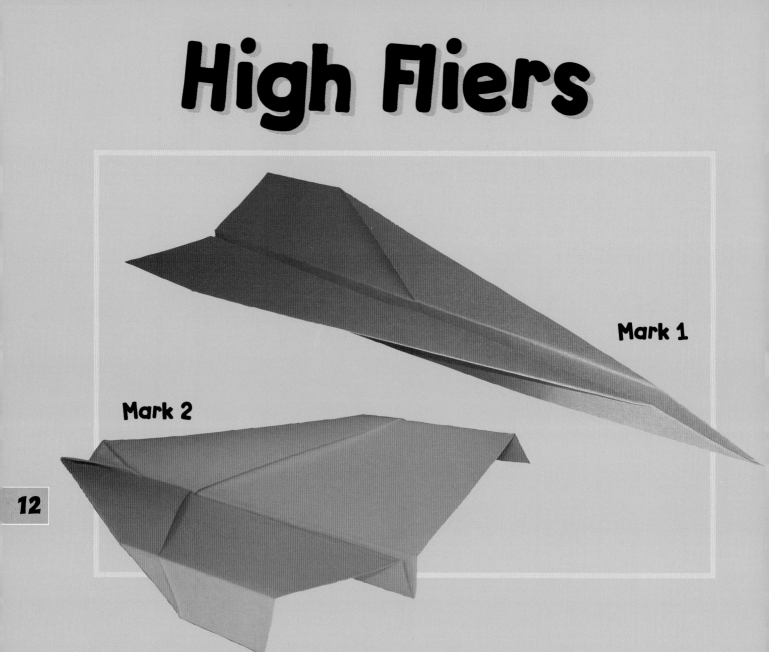

Mark 1

Mark 2

You may know how to make the Mark 1, but what about the Mark 2? It has lots more folds, but is it a better flier?

You will need:

- Colored paper or white office paper
- Ruler
- Paper clip

10 MINUTES

What to do...

Work on a desk or table. You need to make sharp folds. Follow steps 1 to 4 for the Mark 1 glider. Go to steps 5 to 9 for the Mark 2. This one should be great!

2 MINUTES

1

Fold the paper lengthwise, crease and open flat.

2

Fold the top corners to the middle, then fold again.

3

Fold the sides into the middle. Go to step 4 for Mark 1, step 5 for Mark 2.

4

Mark 1 only

Fold the wings out 1 inch (25 mm) from the edge.

5

Fold the tip down to touch the point where the folds meet.

6

Fold the sides into the middle.

7

Fold on the dotted lines to make winglets.

8

Fold the wings out .5 inch (12 mm) from the edge.

13

9 Hold the center of the plane. The wings should form a V shape. Add a paper clip to the nose. Adjust the winglets and the angle of the wings for best results. Experiment as much as you like for a perfect flight!

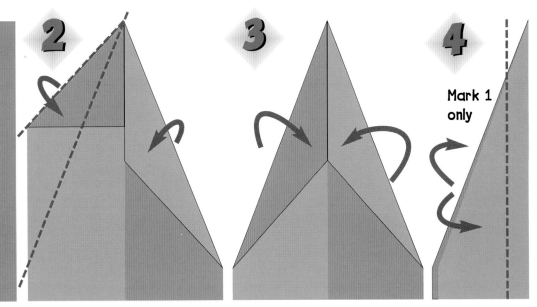

paper clip

cross section of the plane

Party Hats

Party hats are key to getting a party to go well. Follow these easy steps to make a feathered hat and a crown in no time!

You will need:

- Colored paper
- Colored feathers, star stickers
- Scissors, glue stick, stapler
- Markers, pencil

25 MINUTES

What to do...

For our first hat, we've used paper that's blue on one side and white on the other to make the folding easier to follow. Fold the paper lengthwise to make a crease, then flatten it.

5 MINUTES

1

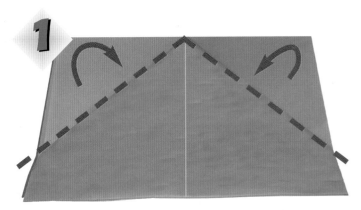

Fold the paper from short side to short side. Fold the corners to meet the center crease.

2

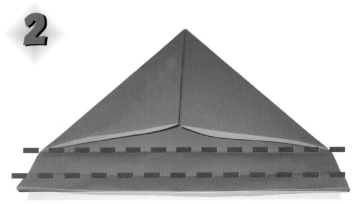

Take the strip below the triangle and fold the top part in half and then up.

3

Turn over, and fold the lower edge as in stage 2. Pull the sides out to form the hat.

4

Make a diamond-shaped badge from paper and a shiny star sticker. Tape some feathers behind it. Glue the badge on.

1

To make a crown, take a piece of paper at least 18 x 5 inches (450 x 125 mm). Fold the length in half and in half again. Draw shapes and cut them out. Staple the ends of the strip together to fit around your head. Glue on colored paper shapes to complete the crown!

2

Paper Flowers

Make five or six of these lovey paper flowers and they will make a colorful arrangement for someone you like.

You will need:

- Colored tissue paper
- Colored crepe paper
- Colored pipe cleaners
- Rubber cement
- Scissors, a pencil

25 MINUTES

What to do...

We're going to make flowers with tissue-paper petals and some colored pipe cleaners for stems. You can experiment with crepe paper as well.

5 MINUTES

1 Fold some squares of tissue paper into quarters. Cut petal shapes out of the unfolded sides. Snip the point off the corner of the folded paper.

2 Open the tissue paper to reveal petal shapes. Cut three different sizes.

3 Fold some squares of green paper and cut into spiky leaf shapes. Snip the point off the corner to make a hole.

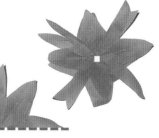

4 Put one of each of the petal shapes on top of each other. Put the spiky leaf shape at the bottom.

5 Use a pipe cleaner for the stem. Fold black tissue into a roll and snip it to make a fringe. Wind this around the top of the stem and glue it on.

6 Push the bottom of the stem down through the holes in the petal shapes. Put glue on the green spiky leaf shape and stick it underneath the petals.

Make leaves from crepe paper. Fix them to the stem with glue.

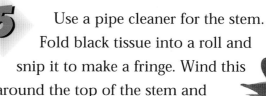

Make the stem form a spiral by winding it around a pencil.

Zigzag Frame

You can easily make a zigzag frame to fit a picture or favorite photo. We've put our paper flowers in a frame!

You will need:

- White card stock
- Colored paper
- Corrugated paper
- Rubber cement
- Scissors, pencil, ruler
- Paper flowers or a picture

30
MINUTES

What to do...

Measure your picture first. Cut the white card stock to size, 5 inches (12 cm) bigger both ways.

5
MINUTES

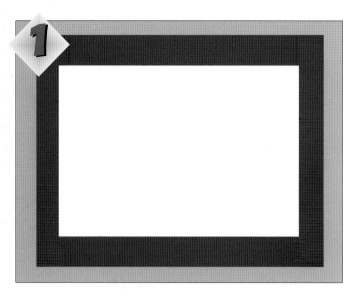

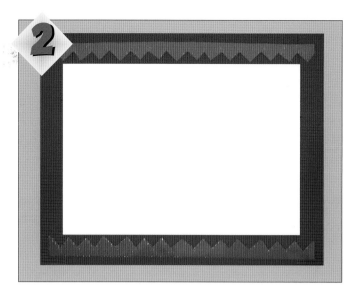

Use corrugated paper or colored paper to make four edge strips. We made ours the same width as our ruler. Glue them to the edges of your white card stock.

Cut another strip of paper in a bright color. Make it twice as wide as the edging and as long as the frame. Mark a zigzag down the strip so that you can cut out two pieces for a border pattern. Stick them to the top and bottom.

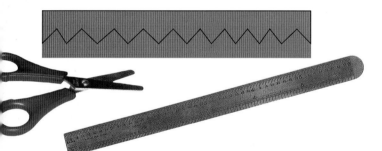

We've used paper flowers from the last activity and arranged them inside the frame.

Stick them down firmly and glue on a simple bowl shape to hide the stems.

Paper Banger!

BANG

These bangers are harmless but can be very noisy! They are easily made from a cereal box and a sheet of office paper. Wow your friends, but remember to keep bangers away from teachers!

10 MINUTES

2 MINUTES

You will need:

- *Empty cereal box*
- *Office paper*
- *Card stock*
- *Marker, ruler*
- *Glue stick*
- *Scissors*
- *Ear plugs (optional)*

What to do...

Our banger is made of two triangles. One is cardboard, measuring 15 x 11 x 11 inches (38 x 27 x 27 cm), and one is paper 11 x 7.5 x 7.5 (27 x 19 x 19 cm) with .5-inch (12 mm) flaps on the short sides. Cardboard from a cereal box is ideal.

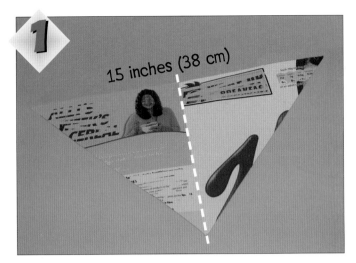

1

15 inches (38 cm)

Carefully fold the cardboard triangle in two.

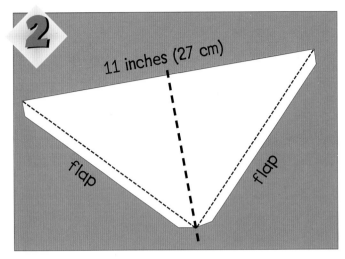

2

11 inches (27 cm)

flap   flap

Cut the paper shape, including flaps. Make the folds as shown.

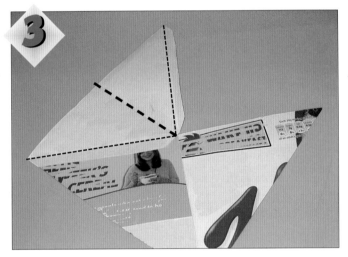

3

Glue one flap of the paper to the matching inner edge of the cardboard.

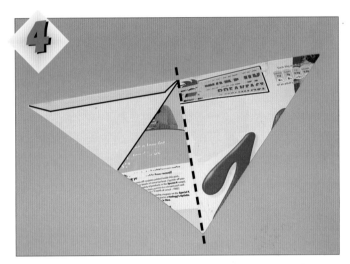

4

Fold the paper in and glue the other flap. Close the cardboard triangle down onto the flap.

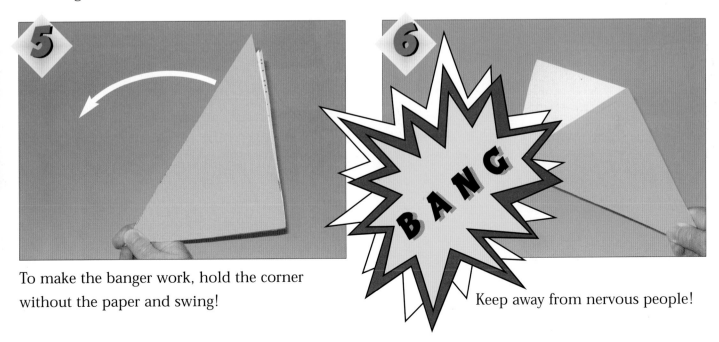

5

To make the banger work, hold the corner without the paper and swing!

6

BANG

Keep away from nervous people!

Snappers

Snappers are quick to make. Once you have the basic shape, it's easy to add different kinds of eyes, eyelashes, nostrils, teeth and tongues. Snappers are spring loaded and can be moved by opening and closing your hand.

15 MINUTES

2 MINUTES

You will need:

- *Colored paper*
- *Scissors*
- *Glue stick*
- *Pencil*

What to do...

Choose some really brightly colored paper to build snappers. Follow the steps 1 to 9. Take care to make sharp folds as you create your snapper. You could work with your friends to see who can make the best snapper!

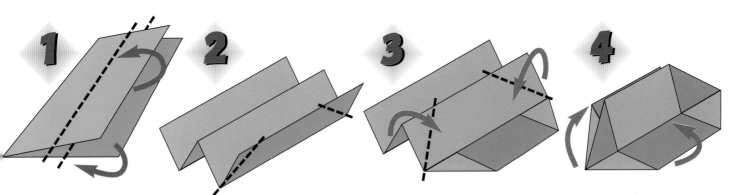

1 Use a square of paper about 8 x 8 inches (20 x 20 cm). Fold it in half, open out, then fold the sides back to the middle.

2 Fold over the corners of the first section to meet the first fold.

3 Fold over the corners of the second section to meet the same fold.

4 Fold over the corners of the last section to meet the fold on that side. Bring the sides up.

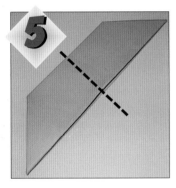
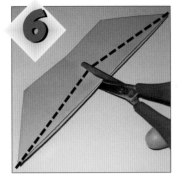

5 Fold the shape in half to find the center.

6 Make a .5-inch (12 mm) cut along the fold through both sides.

7 Fold the long triangles back on both sides.

8 Pull the sides apart.

23

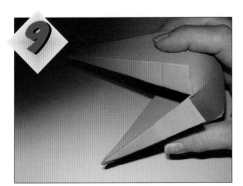
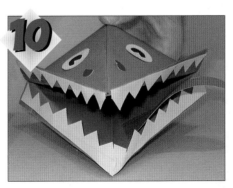

9 Fold it over so that the points meet.

10 Open and close the snapper by moving your fingers and thumb. Stick on eyes, zigzag teeth, nostrils and tongue.

Give your snapper different features to make him special.

Fortune Teller

This fortune teller will be popular, as most people are curious about their future! Write some really interesting fortunes for your friends and family.

You will need:

- Colored or white office paper
- Scissors, ruler
- Marker
- Colored stickers

10 MINUTES

What to do...

You need a square of paper about 8 x 8 inches (20 x 20 cm). Follow steps 1 to 5 carefully and you will soon have a fun object to amuse your friends with.

0 MINUTES

1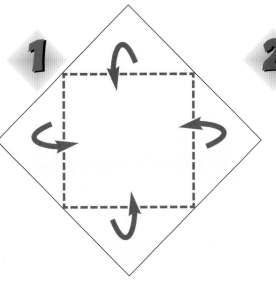

Fold the corners of your paper to the middle.

2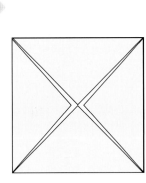

This makes a smaller square. Now turn the paper over.

3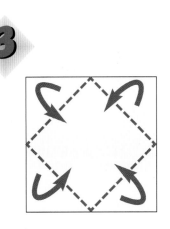

Fold the new corners over into the middle, as before.

4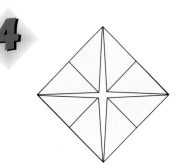

Keep the paper folded and turn it over. You should see four square flaps.

5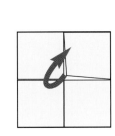

Lift the flaps and put your fingers and thumbs inside to bring the four points together. (See main picture opposite.)

6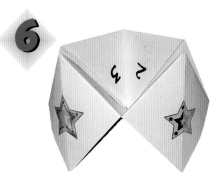

Put on the colored stickers. Write the numbers 1 to 8 and eight messages inside.

7

Ask your friend to choose a color and a number.

8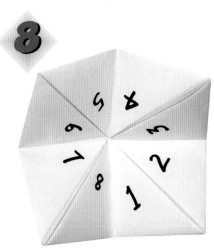

Open and close the fortune teller with your fingers and thumbs, counting to the number.

9

Open at the chosen number and read off their fortune!

Water Bomb!

You can fill this paper box with water and throw it at a friend on a hot day!
It will take you two minutes to make and you don't need glue!

You will need:

- *Colored office paper*
- *Scissors, ruler*
- *Tap water*

2
MINUTES

What to do...

Cut your paper into squares.
An 8 x 8-inch (20 x 20 cm)
square is a good size to start with.
It will make a water bomb a bit
smaller than a tennis ball.

?
MINUTES

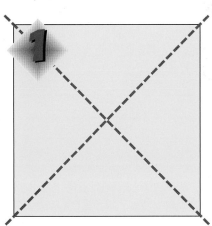

1

Fold your square of paper corner to corner both ways.

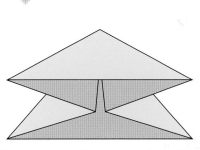

2

Push the sides in so that the paper folds on the creases, making a triangular shape.

3

Fold the corners of the top part up to the middle point.

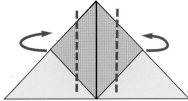

4

Fold over the corners of the flaps to meet in the middle.

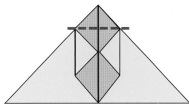

5

Fold down the top points of the triangle.

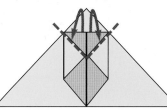

6

Fold the small triangles over and tuck them into the folds.

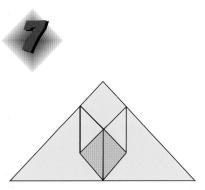

7

Turn the paper over and repeat steps 3 to 6.

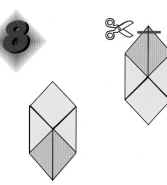

8

Turn the paper upside down and snip or tear off the tip of the point made up of folds.

9

Blow air into the bomb to inflate it. Fill the bomb with tap water and you are ready!

Swan Mobile

25 MINUTES

5 MINUTES

You will need:

- White card stock, scissors, glue stick
- Thin barbecue skewer–8 inches (20 cm)
- Office paper, photocopies, tracing paper, a pin
- Dark thread, black and colored markers

What to do...

You can trace or photocopy our templates on page 30.

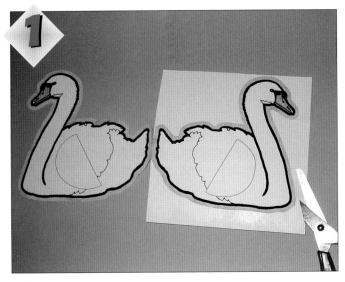

1

Glue a photocopy of the big double swan to card stock, or draw the large swan on both sides of a piece of white card stock. Work in pencil, then go around the edge in thick black marker. Cut the swans out, leaving a border, which you can color pale blue. Color their beaks orange.

2 Cut two wing shapes for each swan from white office paper, using the templates on page 30.

Make four cuts in each wing along the fine lines. Curl the paper by wrapping each strip around a pencil. Make sure your wings are in pairs, left and right. Glue the rounded part of the wings onto the outlined spots on the swan.

3

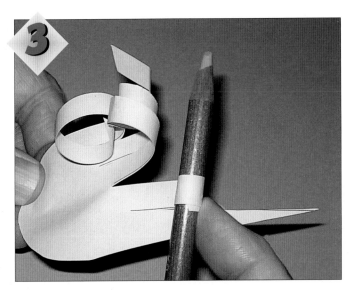

Repeat the steps until you have one large swan and at least three smaller ones. A dot on the top of the swan's back shows where the thread should be fixed. Allow plenty of thread for each swan. Connect the big swan to the middle of the stick using a short thread.

4

Make a hole with a pin and connect a thread. Tie a knot.

Hang one smaller swan at each end of the stick. Put the last swan in the middle, but hanging lower. Make sure all the swans can move freely. Ask an adult to help you. Check the picture on the opposite page.

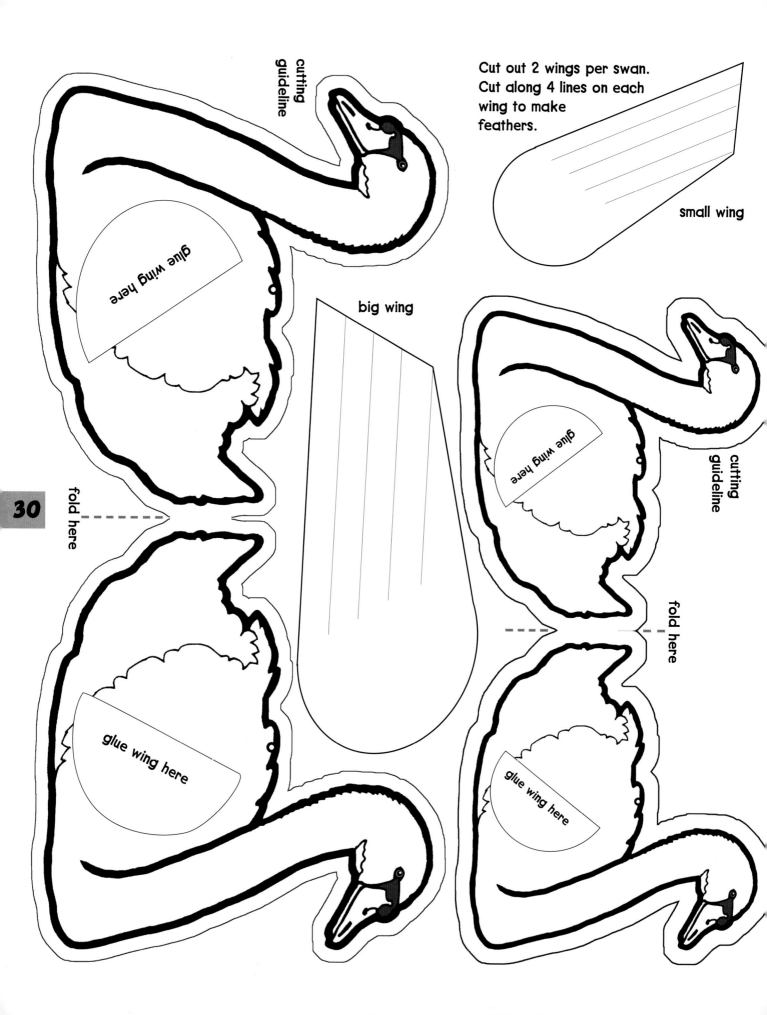

cutting guideline

Cut out 2 wings per swan.
Cut along 4 lines on each wing to make feathers.

small wing

glue wing here

big wing

glue wing here

cutting guideline

fold here

fold here

30

glue wing here

glue wing here

Glossary

cardboard — (KAHRD-bord) Boxes for packaging are made of cardboard. It's often dull grey or brown.

corrugated paper — (KOR-uh-gayt-ed PAY-per) A special kind of cardboard made from two pieces of paper with a wavy piece of paper glued between them. It's a very strong kind of paper.

crease — (KREES) A crease is the mark left by folding card stock or paper and flattening it out again.

crepe paper — (KRAYP PAY-per) This is a special kind of craft paper made with lots of little wrinkles in it. You can pull it into curved shapes like flower petals.

designs — (dih-ZYNZ)   Plans for the form of something.

diagonal — (dy-A-guh-nul)   A diagonal is a line that joins the corners of a square or rectangle.

diamond-shaped — (DY-uh-mund-shaypd) Four sided and pointed at the top and bottom and at both sides.

31

mobile — (MOH-beel) A mobile is an artwork that can move. It's often made to hang from the ceiling.

pipe cleaner — (PYP KLEE-ner) It used to be used to clean smokers' pipes. Now there are colored ones for craft work.

staple — (STAY-pul) A wire fastener you use to fix paper together.

triangle

template — (TEM-plut) Sometimes called a pattern, a template is a guide for making lots of things the same shape. There are some on the opposite page!

tissue paper — (TIH-shoo PAY-per) You can buy colored tissue paper from craft shops. Tissue paper is very thin and is also used for keeping breakable things safe.

tracing paper — (TRAYS-ing PAY-per) Thin but strong paper you can see through. Put it on top of something you want to copy and draw on it.

triangle — (TRY-ang-gel) A guide you use to make sure angles are 90°.

Index

32

Web Sites

Due to the changing nature of Internet links, PowerKids Press has developed an online list of Web sites related to the subject of this book. This site is updated regularly. Please use this link to access the list:
www.powerkidslinks.com/myoa/paper/